the countryside

Translation: Jean Grasso Fitzpatrick

First English language edition published
1986 by Barron's Educational Series, Inc.

The title of the Spanish edition is *el campo*

All inquiries should be addressed to:
Barron's Educational Series, Inc.
250 Wireless Boulevard
Hauppauge, New York 11788
Library of Congress Catalog Card No. 86-7993

International Standard Book No.
Paper: 0-8120-3701-4
Hardcover: 0-8120-5749-X

Library of Congress Cataloging-in-Publication Data

Rius, María.
    Let's discover the countryside.

    (Let's discover series)
    Translation of: *El Campo.*
    Summary: Describes the fields, gardens, crops,
livestock, and processes involved in agriculture and
the chores and general lifestyle of a farming family.
    1. Agriculture—Juvenile literature. 2. Farm
life—Juvenile literature. [1. Agriculture. 2. Farm
life]
I. Parramón, José María. II. Title. III. Series.
S519.F5713   1986   630   86-7993
ISBN 0-8120-5749-X
ISBN 0-8120-3701-4 (pbk.)

234   9760   7654

let's discover
the
countryside

María Rius   J. M. Parramón

BARRON'S

When you see fields of
wheat and poppies,

and gardens full of vegetables…

tomatoes, peppers, and cucumbers…

and trees loaded with fruit…

apples, peaches, and plums.

When you see a village and its people...

and hens and ducks
and rabbits…

pigs and cows and lambs.

When you see the vines, the grapes, and the grape harvest…

and tractors plowing the earth...

and the pure white of the snow on the mountains and roads…

and the bright yellow of the
sunflower fields…

and flowers…and butterflies…

You are in the countryside!

THE COUNTRYSIDE

GUIDE FOR PARENTS AND TEACHERS

Look: the vines that today, in the winter, seem to have dried out, will be wine in the autumn. The fields that are barren today will be wheat in the summer.
This is the miracle of agriculture.
This is the law of the countryside.

Life in the countryside

Life in the countryside is centered on raising crops and livestock. The farmer makes money from both of these activities, and they determine what has to be done each day of the year. A day in the life of a country family starts at dawn. First, the animals must be fed, and their corrals and stables must be cleaned. The rest of the family's work is in the fields where they plow, plant seeds, and harvest the things they have grown. A farmer's day ends with the sunset, and the whole family goes to bed early so they can begin again bright and early the next day.

Agriculture

Agriculture is all the things that farmers do to make things grow and to help people use this produce. Even prehistoric man planted seeds for roots and fruit. Since then, farmers have been figuring out better and better ways to grow more food with less work. Even so, in spite of all the modern machines and techniques, the work is very hard and farmers can never be sure of their crop. Bad weather or disease can ruin a good harvest.

The process of cultivation

Before planting the seeds, farmers have to plow the fields. They break up the dirt with a plow pulled by a team of oxen, or more often by a modern tractor. Once the soil is ready, the farmers must plant the seeds, and sometimes they must also put down chemicals—fertilizers or insecticides. These feed the growing shoots and keep bugs and disease from killing them.

When the fruit is fully grown, it is harvested. There is a season for every crop. The grapes are harvested in the fall, olives are beaten down in the winter, and wheat is cut in the summer. Reaping, the name used for harvesting grain, can be done with sickles and scythes. Today, mechanical harvesters that separate the grain from the stalks and tie the straw in bundles are widely used.

Systems of cultivation

When a farmer is deciding the best way to grow crops, two things must be kept in mind: the soil and the climate. Only the right combination of the two will give the best crop since each crop needs special things. Rice needs hot weather and swampy soil. Cotton also needs hot weather, but it needs to grow in dry soil.

There are two different kinds of crops: the unirrigated crop such as wheat or grain, which only needs rainwater; and the irrigated crop, which needs to be watered often by spraying or having water run through special trenches or canals. Vegetables and fruit trees both need lots of water.

Farm animals

Livestock is the other mainstay of farm life. To make money, farmers keep certain kinds of animals that can be used for food or clothing. Cows supply meat and milk. Sheep provide meat, milk, and wool for clothing. Chickens give meat and eggs. Pigs supply meat which can be preserved (made into sausages) and eaten all year round. A farmer's horse is not used for meat or clothing, but is a wonderful worker. The horse can pull a plow or a wagon, and also carry things on its back. Often, we see sheep grazing in orchards or on mountain slopes. They are watched over by a shepherd. The shepherd has one or two clever dogs who help him keep the sheep from wandering off and getting lost.

Life in the country is, despite its bucolic reputation, extremely hard. The farmer works the land from sunrise to sunset, takes care of the animals and endures a whole series of discomforts peculiar to this way of life, while for reasons totally beyond human control, such as inclement weather or disease, all the efforts of a whole year can end in failure.